# An American Army of Two

### by Janet Greeson

illustrations by
### Patricia Rose Mulvihill

Carolrhoda Books, Inc. / Minneapolis

*For Pete and Lucille*

I would like to thank the Scituate Historical Society at the Little Red School House in Scituate for its extensive help on researching this project. Since *An American Army of Two* is an imaginative retelling of a historical event, the society cannot endorse it or any other such work as the authoritative version. But the society has been generous in providing me with counsel and the content of primary sources, and I am extremely grateful. Also, special thanks to Thomas Shaw of the Minnesota Historical Society at Fort Snelling, Professor Chalon Ragsdale of the University of Arkansas, in Fayetteville, and my relatives in Boston—Joe, Jenny, and Joe Lee. ~ *J. G.*

Thank you to the Tully family for their patience, good humor, and hot tea. ~ *P. R. M.*

*This book is available in two editions:*
Library binding by Carolrhoda Books, Inc.
Soft cover by First Avenue Editions
c/o The Lerner Group
241 First Avenue North
Minneapolis, Minnesota 55401

Text copyright © 1992 by Janet Greeson.
Illustrations copyright © 1992 by Carolrhoda Books, Inc.

Library of Congress Cataloging-in-Publication Data

**Greeson, Janet, 1952-**
     An American army of two / by Janet Greeson; illustrations by Patricia Mulvihill.
     p. cm. — (A Carolrhoda on my own book)
     Summary: During the War of 1812, Rebecca and Abigail Bates save their town's ships from the British by playing "Yankee Doodle" on a fife and drum to simulate the approach of American troops.
     ISBN 0-87614-664-7 (lib. bdg.)
     ISBN 0-87614-547-0 (pbk.)
     1. United States—History—War of 1812—Juvenile fiction [1. United States—History—War of 1812—Fiction.] I. Mulvihill, Patricia, ill. II. Title. III. Series.
PZ7.G8536Am 1991
[E]—dc20                                                                                    90-23194
                                                                                                    CIP
                                                                                                    AC
Manufactured in the United States of America
2  3  4  5  6  7  -  P/SP  -  00  99  98  97  96  95

# Author's Note

The history of the War of 1812 is full of famous stories of brave American soldiers. Yet few soldiers served their country more courageously than the two Bates sisters, Rebecca and Abigail.

Rebecca Bates was born in 1793. In this same year, France and Great Britain went to war. The United States tried not to enter their fight. But Great Britain was kidnapping American sailors and blocking the United States from trading with Europe. So in June 1812, President Madison asked Congress to declare war on England.

The war lasted three years. Most battles happened at sea, on the shores of the Great Lakes or the eastern Atlantic Ocean, or on major American rivers. British troops came by ship or marched from forts in the British territories of Canada.

People in New England were hit hard by the war. They had troubles getting supplies, and they were afraid of being attacked. The soldiers who protected them were usually part-time volunteers. The volunteer soldiers fought as members of their state's troops—the Home Guards.

Fifers and drummers were important members of these troops and the regular army. On a battlefield filled with smoke and gunfire, a captain's commands could not be heard. So the fifers and drummers played songs to let the soldiers know the captain's orders—*March! Charge! Wake up! Retreat!* These musicians had a difficult and dangerous job. Many times the soldiers in their company disliked them for giving orders, and the enemy shot at them to stop commands.

Rebecca and Abigail Bates played a small part in the War of 1812 by using a fife and a drum. There are many different stories about how and when they did this. In *An American Army of Two,* I present Rebecca's story and facts that were found in more than one early source. These sources state that the British were in the Scituate area of Massachusetts for two successful attacks—one on June 11 and one on July 7, 1814. The events of this story are thought to have occurred that summer, when Rebecca was 20 years old and Abigail was 16.

The Scituate lighthouse still stands, and visitors are welcome. The graves of Rebecca and Abigail Bates can be found at Union Cemetery in Scituate.

It was a clear morning in 1814.
The bright July sun shone through
the tall lighthouse windows.

Rebecca Bates polished
the lighthouse lamps.
Abigail, Rebecca's younger sister,
trimmed the wicks.
Their father filled the lamps with oil.
Abigail looked out at the ocean.
The sun made the water sparkle.

"I see two little dots," she said.

"They're ships," Mr. Bates said.

Rebecca came up behind her father.

"Are they British?" she asked.

"They're too far away to tell," he said.

"I hope they aren't," Abigail said.
"They might burn the boats in the harbor,
like they did before."
"Don't worry, Nabby," Mr. Bates said.
"The ships have to anchor
near Cedar Point to get into the harbor,
and we'll see them.
If they *are* British,
we'll send someone for help."
Rebecca, Abigail, and Mr. Bates
watched the ships.
They saw the Union Jack,
the flag of Great Britain.
It was flying from the top
of the ships' masts.
The ships sailed toward Cedar Point.

Mr. Bates, Rebecca, and Abigail
ran down the tower stairs.
They jumped into
one of the lighthouse boats
and rowed to the town wharf.

"The British will be here soon,"
they yelled.
Townspeople came running.
"What shall we do?" a man asked.
"I say we fight!" a young woman shouted.
"We're not soldiers," Mr. Bates said.
"The British have guns and cannons,
but we don't."

Some townsfolk ran to their homes.
They tied dishes, cooking pans,
and food in sheets and tablecloths.
Then they hid them so the soldiers
couldn't steal them.
Other people watched the British ships
and argued about what to do.
One man rode out of town to look
for the Massachusetts Home Guard.

The British ships stopped
near Cedar Point and dropped anchor.
Rowboats were lowered into the water.
Soon British soldiers in bright red coats
stood on the town wharf.
They held their guns close to their sides.

"Lobsterbacks!" Abigail whispered.
The soldiers marched
toward the townspeople.
Rebecca moved closer to her father.
Abigail grabbed his hand and held it tight.
"We want meat, vegetables, and
fresh water," the British officer said.
"No," said Mr. Thomas, the parson.
"We won't give supplies to our enemy."
"Then take their boats,"
the officer ordered his men.
The British soldiers jumped onto some
of the fishing boats tied to the wharf.
The people watched as the soldiers
set one of the boats on fire.
Would their homes be next?

The British soldiers took four boats away.
They also took food and water
from the people of Scituate.
Then the red-coated soldiers
rowed back to their ships.
Mr. Bates, Rebecca,
and Abigail rowed home.
The British ships sailed back and forth
past Cedar Point all that week.
And the next.
And the next.
Sometimes the British soldiers rowed
to town for more supplies.
When would they leave?
the people wondered.

One afternoon, Mr. Bates rowed
to town with some of his children —
Rebecca, Abigail, and the twins.
Mr. Bates wanted to get some news.
But there was none.
The British soldiers were at the wharf,
and no one was saying much.
Rebecca and Abigail decided to walk home.
Maybe some of their neighbors
would know something.

As they walked down the road,
the sisters heard the faint sounds
of a drum and a fife.
"They're playing 'Yankee Doodle,'"
Rebecca said.
"The Home Guard must be coming
to drive the British away," Abigail cried.
"Let's go tell Papa."

The sisters ran back to town.

"Our troops are coming!

Our troops are coming!"

Rebecca and Abigail yelled.

The townspeople heard them yelling.

They ran out of their houses and stores.

Fishermen stopped mending their nets.

Children stopped playing.

The British officer stopped talking
to Parson Thomas.

The officer looked angry.

He walked over to the sisters.

"You're lying," he said.

"No! We're not," Rebecca said.

"Listen."

Everyone listened.

They heard "Yankee Doodle"
coming lightly through the trees.
Even the British officer knew
the American soldiers' marching tune.
"So your troops are coming," he said.
"We came to rest, not to fight.
We'll return when they are gone."
The soldiers rowed back to their ships
and sailed away.

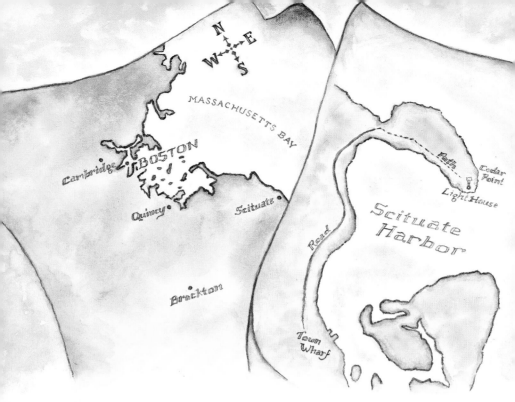

The townspeople cheered as the troops
of the Massachusetts Home Guard
marched into town.
But the American soldiers
could not stay long.
Miles and miles lay along
the Massachusetts coast.
The Home Guard had to watch every mile.

In less than a week,
the American soldiers marched out of town.
One man stayed at the lighthouse
as a guard.
The guard was to ride for the troops
if he saw a British ship.

Rebecca and Abigail went
to meet the guard.

His name was Levi.

"Are you a fifer?" Rebecca asked.

She pointed to the wooden pipe
in Levi's pocket.

"Yes," Levi said. "I play the drum too,
but not at the same time."

He smiled.

"Fifers and drummers
go with the officers into battle."

Levi handed Rebecca the fife.

"Here, try it," he said.

"Hold the fife out to the side.

Then make your lips tight
and blow across the hole."

Rebecca brought the pipe to her mouth
the way Levi showed her.

She tightened her lips and blew.

Out came a high squeak.

Abigail laughed.

It didn't sound anything like

"Yankee Doodle."

Then Levi pulled a drum
and two drumsticks from his pack.
He handed them to Abigail.
"Hold the sticks this way," Levi said.
"Put your left hand
under one stick, palm up.
Put your right hand over
the other stick, palm down," he said.
Abigail held the drumsticks just right.
She banged them up and down
on the drum, fast and hard.
"Slow down!" Levi said, grinning.
"Troops can't march that fast."

Weeks passed.

The British didn't come back.

Rebecca and Abigail practiced
the fife and the drum.

Soon they could play "Yankee Doodle"
almost as well as Levi.

Early one morning, Rebecca and Abigail
were making corn bread with their mother.
"I wish we had sugar," Abigail said.
"I'm tired of using boiled pumpkin
to make things taste better."
"You may get your wish, Nabby,"
Mrs. Bates said.
"Last night, two supply ships
slipped into the harbor.
Your father took the other children with Levi
to see what the ships have to sell.
If there is sugar and flour,
they'll bring some home."
The sisters cheered.
"Now go do your lighthouse chores,"
Mrs. Bates said, smiling.
"I'll finish the corn bread."

Rebecca and Abigail climbed
the stairs to the top of the tower.
Quickly, they ran back down.

"Mama, the British are back!" Abigail cried.
"We just saw a British ship anchored off
Cedar Point!" Rebecca said.
"You and Abigail stay here,"
Mrs. Bates said. "Keep a lookout.
I'll find Levi and send him for
the Home Guard."
Mrs. Bates ran out the door.

"What if they burn
the supply ships, Becky?
What if they burn the town?"
Abigail asked.

Rebecca ran toward the lighthouse stairs.
She stopped when she saw
Levi's fife and drum.

"We won't let the British burn our town,"
Rebecca said. "Here."
She handed Abigail the drum.

"You take the drum.
I'll take the fife."

"Where are we going?" Abigail asked.

"To fight the British," Rebecca said.
"Come on!"

"With a fife and drum?" Abigail asked.
She held the drum but didn't move.
"They'll hurt us," she cried.

"They won't see us," Rebecca said.

"If they don't see us, they can't hurt us."

Rebecca grabbed Abigail's hand and ran.

The sisters ran to the edge of Cedar Point.
They hid behind the thick cedar trees.
Abigail moaned when she saw the British
send off two rowboats of soldiers
in bright red coats.
"They have guns!" she said.
"Shhh," hissed Rebecca.

The soldiers rowed toward the harbor.

"They're getting so close,"
Abigail whispered.

"They're not close enough to hear music,"
Rebecca whispered back.

Abigail gripped the drumsticks tight
to keep her hands from shaking.

The soldiers were getting too close.

They would see her and Rebecca!

"Now, Nabby!" Rebecca whispered.

"Play soft at first.

Then play louder.

We have to make them think

our troops are coming."

Rebecca licked her dry lips

and took a deep breath.

Abigail held the drumsticks

left palm up, right palm down.

Rebecca nodded,

and they started to play.

At first, "Yankee Doodle"
sounded shaky and weak.
But they played the tune again and again.
Each time, the sisters played
louder and stronger.

The music floated over the water
toward the British soldiers.
Suddenly, they stopped rowing
and listened.
One of the soldiers raised his gun
and looked toward the cedar trees.

The two sisters scrunched lower.

Is he going to shoot us?

they wondered.

Abigail's hands were tired.

Rebecca was short of breath.

But they made themselves play louder.

Then the officer
in the first rowboat stood up.
"Turn around!" he shouted.
"American troops are coming."
Slowly, the soldiers turned the boats
and rowed back toward their ship.
"We did it, Becky! We did it!"
Abigail exclaimed in a whisper.
Rebecca was too out of breath to talk.
And her lips were
too numb from playing to smile.
But it wasn't over yet.
The officer could change his mind.

The sisters kept playing.
Finally, all the red-coated soldiers
were back on their ship.
Rebecca and Abigail watched the ship
sail away until it was just
a little dot on the ocean.

The sisters ran back to the lighthouse.
"Becky! Nabby!" Mrs. Bates called.
"Where were you?" Mr. Bates asked.
"We scared the British away!"
Rebecca cried.
"What?" everyone asked at once.

The sisters told them
how they had tricked the British.
"You tricked us too," Mr. Bates said.
"We heard the music, but we thought
it was from the Home Guard."
The sisters smiled proudly.

"Where's Levi?" Rebecca asked.
"I want to give him his fife."
"And his drum," Abigail added.
"Levi rode to get the Home Guard,"
Mrs. Bates said.
"But we don't need them now.
We've got you,
an American army of two!"

# Afterword

"Yankee Doodle" has been called "the old air from nobody-knows-where." No one is quite sure where and when the tune was first played. Some scholars think it began during the Middle Ages as a European march or folkdance. Others think it came from an English nursery rhyme called "Lucky Locket Lost Her Pocket."

Historians, however, *are* sure that "Yankee Doodle" became very popular during the Revolutionary War. At the beginning of the war, British soldiers sang the song as an insult to the untrained Americans who had no uniforms and didn't care to march in straight lines. *Yankee* meant an ordinary man; *doodle* meant a silly fellow who was lazy (a do-little); and a *dandy* (as well as a *macaroni*) was a man who liked to dress with fancy frills—ribbons, feathers, and bows.

American troops liked the lively, easy-to-march-to song. Soon they were playing it for themselves as they marched into battle. By the end of the Revolutionary War, in 1783, the British hated the song and never wanted to hear it again. But they heard it many times during the War of 1812.

After this war, a time of peace and respect began between the United States and England. In 1819, a ball was given in Washington, D. C., to honor a visiting British official. The band played the English national anthem, "God Save the King." When the song was over, the Englishman wanted the band to play something for the Americans. But the United States did not have a national anthem yet. So the British official asked the band to play "Yankee Doodle."

Throughout the years, "Yankee Doodle" has remained an American favorite. It was the first patriotic song of the United States, and it may well be the only Revolutionary War song we still sing.

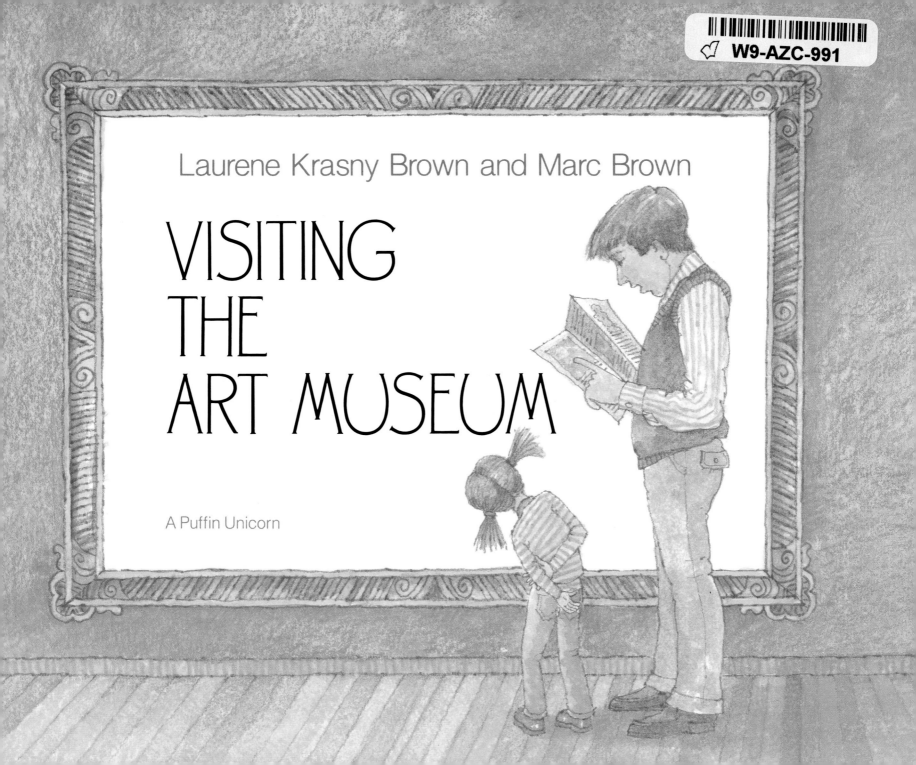

Laurene Krasny Brown and Marc Brown

# VISITING THE ART MUSEUM

A Puffin Unicorn

Cover art credits are on page 32.

Copyright © 1986 by Laurene Krasny Brown and Marc Brown

All rights reserved.

Unicorn is a registered trademark of Dutton Children's Books.

Library of Congress number 85-32552
ISBN 0-14-054820-3

Published in the United States by Dutton Children's Books,
a division of Penguin Books USA Inc.

Editor: Ann Durell    Designer: Isabel Warren-Lynch

Printed in Hong Kong by South China Printing Co.
First Unicorn Edition 1990
10  9  8  7

3

5

9

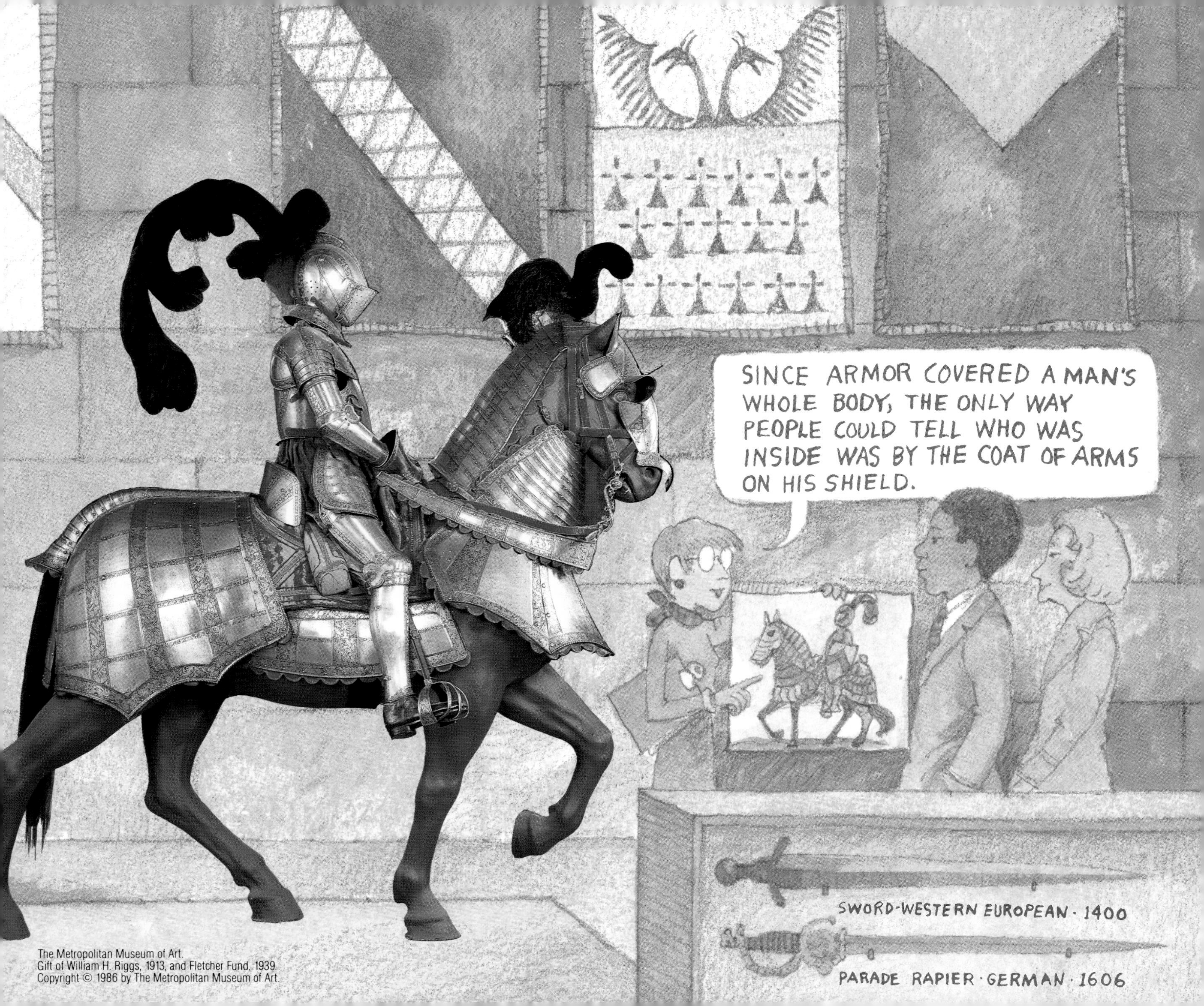

SINCE ARMOR COVERED A MAN'S WHOLE BODY, THE ONLY WAY PEOPLE COULD TELL WHO WAS INSIDE WAS BY THE COAT OF ARMS ON HIS SHIELD.

SWORD·WESTERN EUROPEAN·1400

PARADE RAPIER·GERMAN·1606

15

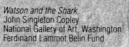

LOOK AT THE TEETH ON THIS SHARK! THAT MAN WILL LOSE MORE THAN HIS CLOTHES.

DON'T FEEL BAD, ROSIE. THE MAN OVERBOARD WAS SAVED. HE LIVED TO BECOME LORD MAYOR OF LONDON.

IT'S A MEAN PICTURE. I HATE IT!

17

18

19

Rousseau, Henri.
*The Sleeping Gypsy.* 1897.
Oil on canvas, 51" x 6'7".
Collection, The Museum of Modern Art, New York.
Gift of Mrs. Simon Guggenheim.

MOMMY, LOOK AT THIS LION. HE WHISPERS, "WATCH OUT OR I'LL EAT YOU UP!" BUT SHE DOESN'T HEAR HIM.

BECAUSE SHE'S SLEEPING. WHAT DO YOU THINK SHE IS DREAMING ABOUT?

THIS WAS PAINTED BY HENRI ROUSSEAU. HE NEVER STUDIED ART. HE TAUGHT HIMSELF TO PAINT.

MAYBE THERE'S HOPE FOR ME.

20

21

Pollock, Jackson (American, 1912–1956)
*Portrait and a Dream*
1953
PAINTING enamel on canvas
H 58⅛" x W 134¼"
1967.8
Dallas Museum of Art, gift of Mr. and Mrs. Algur H. Meadows and the Meadows Foundation Incorporated

22

23

24

25

# MORE ABOUT THE ART

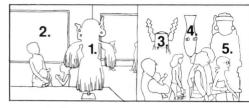

pages 6–7

## PRIMITIVE GALLERY

The word *primitive* refers to the art of those people who, over the years, have done their work using tools but no modern machines. Primitive artists have no formal schooling in art. People in countries all over the world have made primitive art.

**1.** This costume was constructed in the 1900s by the Asmat people of Irian Jaya, New Guinea. To make it, they used natural materials such as palm leaves, rattan, seeds, feathers, and wood.

**2.** Based on a painting of crocodiles and wallabies, made on tree bark by the Banjo of Umba Kumba, Australia

**3.** Based on a Katchina mask painted on leather by Zuni Indians of southwest America

**4.** Based on a mask carved from wood by the Grebo, a seagoing tribe of Ivory Coast, Africa

**5.** Based on a stone warrior made by the Toltecs of Mexico

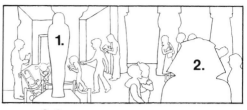

pages 8–9

## ANCIENT EGYPTIAN GALLERY

Even though its culture ended almost two thousand years ago, a lot is known about life in ancient Egypt. One reason is that the Egyptians preserved in their tombs many possessions which they expected to use in their life after death. The Egyptians also took great care with burying people.

**1.** This mummy case was made to hold the body of a woman named Tabes. She was the singer at the Temple of Amun, and her husband was the barber there. Her mummy must still be inside, because the case has not been opened since it was sealed in about 940 B.C.

**2.** Based on a sculpture of Pharaoh Thutmose III. During his reign, Thutmose conquered many foreign neighbors and added their lands to Egypt's empire.

pages 10–11

## CLASSICAL GREEK AND ROMAN GALLERY

Greek artists were the first to make sculptures of people and animals that looked almost as natural as living beings. The Greeks studied the body's structure, or anatomy, to learn where the muscles and bones were and how they worked.

**1.** This marble *Discus Thrower* is a Roman copy of a Greek statue made in about 450 B.C. Discus throwing was one event at early Olympic Games, along with chariot races, boxing, and many other sports. But at the first Olympics, there was only one event, a running race. The length of this race, 630 feet, is said to have been the distance Hercules could walk while holding his breath.

**2.** Based on a Greek sculpture made in the 400s B.C.

**3.** Based on a vase painted by Psiax, a Greek artist, in about 525 B.C. The picture shows Hercules strangling the Nemean lion.

pages 12–13

## ARMS AND ARMOR GALLERY

Warriors in the 500s to 1500s wore armor to protect their bodies during battle. The knight was a warrior with enough money to own a horse and enough means to keep his followers well cared for and safe.

**1.** This man's battle armor was made by French metalworkers in about 1550. The horse's armor is from Italy. A knight on horseback, wearing armor like this, would carry a long lance, a sword, and a steel club or mace. Then in the 1600s, pistols became popular and began to replace both armor and lances.

**2.** Based on parade armor made for the French king Henry II. It might take a skilled metalworker two years to fashion armor as fancy as this.

**3.** Based on Italian armor made in about 1400. The sleeveless jacket is soft velvet on the outside, but it has steel plates on the inside.

pages 14–15

## RENAISSANCE GALLERY

The word *renaissance* means rebirth in French. Between the 1300s and 1500s, artists realized they could learn a lot by looking back in history to classical Greek and Roman times. For example, Renaissance artists revived the practice of showing people and other living things in a realistic way.

**1.** This painting, *The Battle of San Romano,* by Paolo di Dono (known as Uccello) tells about an actual battle fought between Florentines and Sienese in Italy in 1432. The Florentine captain is the man in the center riding a white horse. By the way, his side won.

**2.** Based on a painting, *Saint George and the Dragon,* by Raffaello Sanzio (known as Raphael), dated 1504–05. Saint George is said to have killed dragons in England, Germany, and even Africa.

**3.** Based on the sculptor Donatello's statue of *Saint George,* made from 1415 to 1417.

pages 16–17

## EIGHTEENTH-CENTURY GALLERY

Since cameras were not yet invented by the 1700s, paintings and drawings were the only way to record people, places, and events. Artists made paintings about all sorts of subjects: splendid things, tragic things, and also everyday things.

**1.** This 1778 painting, *Watson and the Shark,* by John Singleton Copley, re-creates an accident—when Brook Watson fell overboard in the harbor at Havana, Cuba. He was rescued, but he did lose a leg to the shark. Copley made three different paintings of this scene.

**2.** Based on a portrait of a Spanish count's son, painted by Francisco Goya in 1787. Goya was the official painter of the king of Spain.

**3.** Paul Revere, the famous American patriot and silversmith, made all his pieces by hand, carefully hammering the silver into shapes of teapots, mugs, and other useful things.

pages 18–19

### IMPRESSIONIST GALLERY

According to a group of French artists working in the 1870s, artists should depict the world as they see it, using whatever style they want. Many of these Impressionist artists chose to paint or sculpt subjects from circuses, dance halls, and other places of entertainment.

**1.** Pierre-Auguste Renoir painted this picture, *Two Little Circus Girls,* in 1879. He liked to show people in their own surroundings, doing what they usually did, not posed and stiff in the artist's studio. Renoir got his first job when he was thirteen years old, painting designs on porcelain plates.

**2.** Based on a painting, *The Bath,* done in 1891 by Mary Cassatt. Cassatt was the first important woman artist born in America, though she lived and worked in Paris when she grew up.

**3.** Based on a sculpture, *Little Dancer Aged Fourteen,* made by Edgar Degas between 1880 and 1881.

pages 20–21

### POST-IMPRESSIONIST GALLERY

Post-Impressionist painters wanted even more freedom to express themselves than the Impressionists.

**1.** This picture, called *The Sleeping Gypsy* and painted in 1897, looks like a mysterious scene in some far-off desert. Yet the artist, Henri Rousseau, lived in the city of Paris. Rousseau liked painting wild animals—especially lions, tigers, and monkeys—and he often visited these animals at the zoo.

**2.** Based on Vincent van Gogh's painting from 1889, *The Starry Night.* Van Gogh worked hard to show his emotions in his art. Perhaps he wanted us to known from this painting how exciting it is to feel the wind and see bright stars light up the sky.

**3.** Based on the still-life painting, *Apples and a Pot of Primroses,* by Paul Cezanne, dated 1890–94. Cezanne arranged things very carefully to make a pleasing design of different shapes.

pages 22–23

### TWENTIETH CENTURY, ABSTRACT GALLERY

Paintings don't have to show a recognizable person, place, or thing to be considered art. Artists sometimes use paintings and sculpture to express an idea or a feeling, or even to tell something about how they do their artwork.

**1.** Jackson Pollock made paintings like this one, *Portrait and a Dream,* dated 1953, not only by applying paint with a brush but also by pouring it right on the canvas. Some people call his work action painting. Can you see why?

**2.** Based on a 1921 cubist painting, *The Three Musicians,* by Pablo Picasso. Even though Picasso could draw realistic figures, he chose to depict these musicians by arranging shapes of different color paint.

**3.** Based on a mobile, *Lobster Trap and Fish Tail,* made by Alexander Calder in 1939. Mobiles are constructed to move with the slightest breeze.

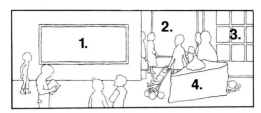

pages 24–25

## TWENTIETH CENTURY, POP GALLERY

In the 1960s, artists began using popular images from products, advertising, and the mass media as subjects for their artwork. These pop artists picture commonplace things about life, but show them to you in new and different ways. Since pop art is recent, many artists whose work appears in this gallery are still alive and doing new art.

**1.** Roy Lichtenstein painted *Whaam!* in 1963. He even decorates his own surroundings with pictures of everyday things: The elevator door to his work studio is painted to look like Swiss cheese!

**2.** Based on a 1966 painting, *Love,* by Robert Indiana

**3.** Based on Andy Warhol's painting, *Campbell's Soup Cans,* painted from 1961 to 1962

**4.** Based on a soft sculpture, *Floor Cake,* made in 1962 by Claus Oldenberg

# TIPS FOR ENJOYING AN ART MUSEUM

- Take your time looking at art. You don't have to see everything on display in one visit.

- Take a break for lunch or some other activity after thirty or forty-five minutes. That way you won't get too tired.

- Wear comfortable shoes (like sneakers).

- Read the label posted near an art object when you want to know the title, artist, date made, and medium used.

- Touching the art is not permitted. Museums try to take care of valuable things and keep them from getting damaged, worn, or dirty.

- Ask at the information desk if there are materials or activities especially for children.

- Go on treasure hunts. Search paintings for things like hats, shoes, faces, hands; boys, girls; different animals. Whoever finds the most examples wins.

- Hunt for such features of art as circles, squares; shadows; certain colors; brushstrokes; different moods—like happy, sad, or mysterious.

- Hunt for sculptures that look smooth or rough.

- Make up stories about what is happening in different paintings. Try to predict what would happen if the picture continued to a next scene.

- Looking at portraits: Choose whom you would want to be your sister, brother, father, mother, or friend.

*continued on page 32*

- Be a detective. Try to figure out what job each person in the painting had, what kind of person each was, etc.
- Decide which artwork in a gallery you like best and which you like least. Explain why.
- Read books on art and artists. There are a number of good ones for children.

A *special thanks* to the people whose helpful advice we have used in this book:

Joyce Black, Linda Cohen, and Kathleen Walsh from the Art Institute of Chicago

Joan Cavanaugh from the Metropolitan Museum of Art, New York

Wendy Baring-Gould, Enid Gifford, and Sally Leahy from the Museum of Fine Arts, Boston

Lynn Russell from the National Gallery of Art, Washington, D.C.